YOUR GIFTS

ARE NOT YOUR

PURPOSE!

by

Laval W. Belle

Caring Ministries

Caring Ministries
5850 West 3rd Street, Suite 353
Los Angeles, California 90036

www.caringministries.com
lwbelle@hotmail.com

Printed in the United States of America
First Printing: March 1998
Second Printing May 2006
1 0 9 8 7 6 5 4 3 2

ISBN 0-9662750-7-1
Rev. August 6, 2006

Dedicated to my mother, Eva Belle,

To the **suicidal** person, don't give up,

To individuals who feel they are a mistake,

To the reader who seeks true
understanding of self,

To every youth seeking direction.

Minster Belle is also the author of:

"LOVE IN ALL THE WRONG FACES"

"THE SAINT AND SEXUAL ADDICTION"

"WHY I DON'T PAY TITHES"

Laval W. Belle

CONTENTS

PREFACE………………………………………………………..vii

INTRODUCTION………………………………………….... x

1. UNDERSTANDING THE GIFT………………………14

2. THE PURPOSE OF THE GIFTS…………………….....24

3. YOUR GIFT CAN BUILD OR DESTROY YOU……..36

4. YOUR GIFTS ARE A VEHICLE TO YOUR PURPOSE
    ……………………………………………………… 70

5. SO WHAT IS PURPOSE?..98

6. GOD'S MULTIPLE PURPOSE………………………110

7. TIME………………………………………………..130

Laval W. Belle

YOUR GIFTS ARE NOT YOUR PURPOSE!

ACKNOWLEDGEMENTS

I'd like to express my gratitude to my Pastor, Bishop Charles E. Blake and to the leaders and friends of the West Angeles C.O.G.I.C. family. I thank God for the positive influence you've had on my life.

I offer my thanks to Pastor David Epley and the Miami Christian Center. Thank you for the endless seeds and opportunities you've planted.

Thanks to Sharon Hogg, Stephanie Shelling and Holli Leonard for your endless encouragement and steadfast **love**.

To Judy McAllister and the West Angeles Bible College — Thanks for your instruction.

To Mother Manor, Elder John Taylor and 6:00 a.m. prayer—you're always there.

BECAUSE OF THESE PEOPLE MY LIFE HAS CHANGED, OTHERS WILL BE BLESSED BECAUSE OF THEIR SACRIFICES.

PREFACE

It's one thing to be unaware of your purpose, but quite **frustrating** when you discover purpose only to find yourself empty and still searching for something. It's possible you have confused your gift with your purpose. The dangers of confusing the two are numerous.

After playing the drums for many years and performing with some of the greatest artists in the world, I found myself empty and searching for **that something**, no matter how many goals I accomplished. Even after being saved and Spirit-filled, the **void** was still present. Then something happened in December 1994 while on a three-week tour in Japan. Phillip Bailey, the artist I performed with, asked if I would lead a bible study. I thought, "**Why me**?" I'd never led a bible study before. His advice was, "**Just teach on what you know**." So I gave it some thought and I began preparing a study on relationships. This was something I felt I knew and was safe and familiar with. I put together a one-page outline and was ready to go.

I drifted to sleep when the Lord awakened me and spoke these words, "Your Gifts Are Not Your Purpose." I wondered why the Lord spoke those words. Then He said, "write these words: **"*Your GiftsAre Not Your Purpose!*"** I was obedient and began praying and asked the Lord to tell me what this meant. Lying prostrate on the floor, I began to reflect on my life.

It made perfectly good sense why the Lord wanted me to write the title, "Your Gifts Are Not Your Purpose"— this was my life. The rest is history and still unfolding. Now the Lord has allowed me to share this message with you.

From that day forward, I began to write for the first time with a sense of **purpose**. God created you and me with instinct or conscience—**saved or unsaved**, we know when we're doing right or wrong. Like a traveler in an unfamiliar city looking for an address, we sense when we've gone too far or made a bad turn and become lost.

We hear of countless people who invest in their careers or talents only to find later that they committed suicide or were confined to an institution. When we confuse our gifts with our purpose, we center our esteem or worth around our talents. In essence, we make the gifts our **god**!

Your Gifts Are Not Your Purpose!

INTRODUCTION

In May of 1993, I was playing drums for a pianist in New York City. We were scheduled to work there from Tuesday through Sunday. One night while I was performing, a well known artist named George Benson came to listen to us play.

On that night, two other great musicians happened to be sitting in—Joe Sample and Nathan East. After the concert, George Benson asked me what I was doing the following month. I replied, "Basically nothing." Then asked if I would like a job playing drums for him. I said "yes."

Shortly thereafter, I left to fulfill a commitment in Paris for ten days, After Paris, I was scheduled to start rehearsing with Mr. Benson seven days later, but something else happened. I got a call to audition with a singer by the name of Bette Midler. Because of the enormous politics that usually surround an artist of her caliber, I was sure they wouldn't choose me for the position. However, I felt it would be in my best interest to at least audition.

Not only was I chosen, but they wanted me to start right away. I went into shock. Little did they know I accepted the position with George Benson. I asked the Midler camp if they would allow me to start the next day. I called the musical director for Bette

Midler that night and explained to him that I was offered a job with George Benson and accepted.

By the way, the Musical Director for Bette Midler (Bobby Lyle) was the artist I was performing with in New York City when Mr. Benson discovered my gift. It really didn't matter to Bobby, he wouldn't take no for an answer.

Imagine—the summer of 1993 the largest secular tours were Madonna, Janet Jackson, Better Midler and Michael Jackson. **Here's my big break**, I thought, and all I have to do is say "yes." But I was confused. I mean very confused. I had given George Benson my word, and his rehearsal would start that Friday. Not only would I be going back on my word, but on such short notice. I loved his music and we hit it off so well; yet, everyone advised me to go with Bette Midler. Midler's camp was paying an enormous amount of money and had great benefits for my career. Only one person advised me not to work with Bette and that was my neighbor and friend, Kevin.

Pressure was mounting and when Thursday afternoon arrived I was driving to Bette Midler's rehearsal full of anxiety and frustration. I stopped the car and began running. I didn't know my destination. I just ran until I came to a railroad track and, in the middle of nowhere, I bowed and prayed on the tracks. Literally, I yelled out, "Lord, tell me what to do!" My greatest nightmare would be to lose both opportunities.

The Lord spoke to me clearly and calmly and said, "When you get to rehearsal (Bette Midler's) and they haven't settled your pay issue, go with George Benson. If they've settled your financial issue, stay with Bette."

After the Lord spoke, for the first time in days I felt a sense of peace. Immediately, I went to rehearsal. As soon as I walked through the door, Bette's manager said the financial matter was settled. I knew I had to stay with Bette, but I wasn't excited because I had to call Mr. Benson and tell him the bad news. It was very difficult, but I had made my decision and had to call him. Two weeks later the worst happened. Mrs. Midler decided she wanted to try someone else. I lost both gigs. I knew the Lord spoke to me on the railroad tracks and knew God couldn't lie. So what happened?

*And we know all things work together for good to those who love God, to those who are called according to His **purpose.***
(Romans 8:28)

It was that ordained experience that caused me to ask the questions that every person must ask— **WHY! WHY! WHY!**

You see, God called me at age 12 to prophetically preach and teach His word. Though I asked why this happened to me, the real questions were: Why have You called me? Why can't I just play the drums? Why isn't this working out?

> *A man's heart plans his way, But the Lord directs his steps.* (Proverbs 16:9)

Chapter 1

UNDERSTANDING THE GIFT

WHAT IS A GIFT?

A gift is something that is given! It's a natural endowment or talent. The root word **"endow"** means to furnish or equip, as with talents or natural gifts.

Your gifts are the part of you that differentiates you from every person on this planet. Your gifts are your natural skills and talents that you were given at conception. Your abilities and your outlook on life determine how you will function and how you are designed. These are connected to your natural abilities and potential. Your gift in essence *is* who you are.

For example, if a person's primary (natural) gift is faith or encouragement, no matter what circumstances may arise, he or she will approach the situation with optimism. Or, if your primary gift is serving, helping for you is second nature.

The gifts are the lens to how we perceive life. Our gifts are what make us unique. There's nothing more unique or fascinating than a mother's love. Her natural instinct is to care, protect, love and

15

provide. No one has to teach a mother these things. They are divinely imparted.

> Jesus' primary gift is love: *Greater love has no one than this, than to lay down one's Life for his friends.* (John 15:13)

> *Before I formed you in the womb I knew you before you were born I sanctified you; I ordained you a prophet to the nations.* (Jeremiah 1:5)

I like to think of the gift this way. Imagine God standing with a basket full of goodies and, before we enter earth's atmosphere we stop at His throne and He passes out gifts. Or, imagine an assembly of storks in heaven, called Destiny, ready for their journey to earth, their last stop before dropping off a life to its mother, is the Lord. And, the sovereign, omnipresent, omniscient, omnipotent God gives the new life a present called talent.

When I was five years old, I would beat on everything in sight. At ages eight and nine I tore branches off trees to make drum sticks and surrounded myself with trash can tops, which I would beat for hours. I couldn't help myself. Even in school, I would beat on table tops. It was instinctive to me. No one figured out that I was a drummer until I asked for a set of drums at age 11 after seeing Buddy Rich play on the Tonight Show with Johnny Carson.

WHAT IS THE SOURCE OF THE GIFTS?

> *Every good gift and every perfect gift is from above, and comes down from the Father of lights, with whom there's no variation or shadow of turning.* (James 1:17)

Every gift comes from the Lord. James also tells us that our gifts are perfect, and they are, because we come from a perfect God. What happens to us when we enter earth's realm of imperfection? Sin has no bearing on our origin; neither does it have bearing on God's purpose.

> *Son of man, take up a lamentation for the king of Tyre, and say to him, Thus says the Lord God; You were the seal of perfection, full of wisdom and perfect in beauty. You were **perfect** in your ways from the day you were created, Till iniquity was found in you.* (Ezekiel 28:12, 15)

The King of Tyre began walking with God, but success puffed him up. He was quite gifted in wisdom, beauty and business, but his success caused him to commit the great sin of idolatry (pride). The King got so wrapped up in himself that he felt he

17

was god. But man's outcome has no **variation** on the nature of God. In other words, our gifts are still of a perfect origin and our gifts are who we are. So the gifts are perfect.

For example:

> If I gave a man a hunting knife for a present and he used the knife to murder someone, nothing is wrong with the knife (gift) or the giver, but it's the receiver of the gift who's polluted. It's still a perfectly good knife for hunting.

> *So God created man in His own image; in the image of God He created him; male and female He created them.* (Genesis 1:27)

When God created Adam and Eve, He created them in His perfect image. Of course, it was our great-grandparents' disobedience that plummeted humanity into its fallen state.

> David said: *I was brought forth in iniquity, and in sin my mother conceived me.* (Psalm 51:5)

But even the sinful heart of man couldn't modify the purpose of the gifts. The primary gifts are still good and pure. James 1:17 says that there's no varying or turning back of God's plans for our gifts. We may stumble and fall, but the gifts and the calling of God are irrevocable (see Romans 11:29).

No matter where you are in this journey, the gifts are still effective. Spirit-filled or demon-possessed, talent affects and attracts everyone.

For example:

> When the secular society wants to raise funds, no matter how people feel about each other (ethnic tension), whether rich or poor, folks will come together by the thousands to experience the talents of athletes, musicians and actors.

The religious world is no different. If the pastor asks the saints to come out for Bible study or prayer meeting, attendance is usually low. The moment you announce an upcoming attraction or celebrity, even if you are selling tickets for the event, church attendance is unusually high. Folks like to be entertained. People haven't changed; there's nothing new under the sun (see Ecclesiastes 1:9).

Remember when God called Moses and sent him to Pharaoh? God used the rod that Moses had to perform ten tricks (plagues) to gain the release of the Hebrews from Pharaoh's control, but before the

Lord could use Moses, he had to perform His signs and wonders for Moses.

> So the Lord said to him, "What is that in your hand?" He said, "A rod," and He said, "Cast it on the ground." So he cast it on the ground, and it became a serpent; and Moses fled from it. Then the Lord said to Moses, "Reach out your hand and take it by the tail (and he reached out his hand and caught it, and it became a rod in his hand)....
> (Exodus 4:2-4)

Pharaoh didn't believe Moses because he had magicians who were able to perform the same tricks:

> Aaron cast down his rod before Pharaoh and before his servants and it became a serpent. But Pharaoh also called the wise men and the sorcerers; so the magicians of Egypt, they also did in like manner with their enchantments. For every man threw down his rod and they became serpents....
> (Exodus 7:10b-12a)

We like entertainment, because entertainment makes us feel good. You seldom turn the television on without running into a psychic program. The psychics tell you what you want to hear. They persuade people to exercise other powers.

People followed Jesus because he performed signs and wonders. He turned water into wine, healed the sick, raised the dead, fed the hungry, and brought peace to the tortured soul. In a world of hopelessness, Jesus knew the value and power of the gifts. Yes, the believer knows the gifts reflect His authority and power, but the unbeliever doesn't. Jesus has to get our attention with something that we can relate to.

> It takes a wise man to win a soul.
> (See Proverbs 11:30)

> *We speak what we know and testify what we have seen, and you don't receive our witness. If I have told you earthly things and you don't believe, how will you believe if I tell you heavenly things?* (John 3:11, 12)

Jesus deals with us where we are. Nothing can alter the effectiveness and authenticity of the gifts.

One of the most popular books in the Bible is the book of Psalm. People have either read or heard some portion of it directly or indirectly. Why are people so attracted to the Psalms? One reason I believe is because the principle author, King David, was a musician and songwriter.

Psalms are songs arranged in poetry. It's the music and lyrics that are so attractive. Music is said to be a universal language. David was the greatest worshiper and praise leader who ever lived.

If you don't believe the gifts are powerful, take the music out of most Spirit-filled charismatic church services and you'll discover just how many people come to hear the Word.

WHAT IS THE GREATEST GIFT?

Our greatest gift is Love manifested in Jesus: *He who doesn't love doesn't know God, for God is love.* (1John 4:8)

> *For God so loved the world that He gave His only begotten Son, that whoever believes in Him should not perish but have everlasting life.* (John 3:16)

It was in love, for love and by love that God created you. God is the best teacher on sharing the gifts. God gave His only Son for you and me. God gave for a specific reason, to win man back from satan. God gave sacrificially. Our salvation cost Jesus His life.

The gift of God is eternal life in Christ Jesus our Lord. (Romans 6:23)

Chapter 2

THE PURPOSE OF THE GIFTS

Therefore He says:

*When He ascended on high, He led captivity captive, and gave gifts to men. And He Himself gave some to be apostles, some prophets, some evangelists and some pastors and teachers, for the **equipping** of the saints for the work of ministry, for the edifying of the Body of Christ.* (Ephesians 4:8, 11, 12)

Equipping – A making fit, preparing, training, perfecting, making fully qualified for service.

Spiritual gifts are for the edifying and nurturing of the church, from the office of the leader to every member (teacher, singer, janitor, usher, missionary) in the Body of Christ.

In practical terms, no one is an island. For example, I had the privilege of working in the capacity of Musical Director for several artists. The Musical Director's responsibility is to put together all the music and personnel for the performance. In essence, I was an extension of the artist. The artist can't perform without help. The artist has to incorporate the various talents of other background singers, musicians, sound technicians and so forth.

25

It took all those **bodies** to make up a show for the needs of one artist.

Likewise, God the Father sent Christ on His behalf, along with the Holy Spirit to empower the gifts of the believer for the single **purpose** of redeeming man to God!

> *Now concerning spiritual gifts, brethren, I don't want you to be ignorant: you know that you were Gentiles, carried away to these dumb idols, however you were led. Therefore I make known to you that no one speaking by the Spirit of God calls Jesus accursed, and no one can say that Jesus is Lord except by the Holy Spirit.*
>
> *There are diversities of gifts, but the same Spirit. There are differences of ministries, but the same Lord. And there are diversities of activities, but it's the same God who works all in all. But the manifestation of the Spirit's given to each one for the profit of all: For to one is given the word of wisdom through the Spirit, to another the word of knowledge through the same Spirit, to another gifts of healings by the same Spirit, to another the working of miracles, to another prophecy, to another discerning of spirits, to another*

different kinds of tongues, to another the interpretation of tongues.

But one and the same Spirit works all these things, distributing to each one individually as He wills.

For as the body is one and has many members, but all the members of that one body, being many, are one body, so also is Christ. (I Corinthians 12:1-12)

Have you ever taken the time to ask God why you're gifted? Paul explains in verses 1 and 2 of this passage that he wants us to understand the purpose of the gifts. The Corinthians, like so many of us today, misunderstood the purpose of the gifts. They abused the gifts for their own motives, pleasures or power. The Creator never intended the gifts to be used impulsively or immorally or for manipulation! God has a purpose for the gifts that He entrusted in you. When someone gives you something, it's usually for a reason. For example, AT&T doesn't give away free calling time or incentives because they are being nice or they like you. Their motive is to persuade you to use their phone service in hopes of your becoming a regular customer. Universities don't award scholarships to minorities or inner city children because they are just being helpful. When they pass out a football, basketball, track or whatever type of scholarship, it's because the student will strengthen the team, draw more attention to the school and increase enrollment (revenue). There's usually a motive behind a gift. Corporations don't hand out gifts or give to charitable organizations to be friendly. It's good public relations and a tax write-off.

HOLY SPIRIT EMPOWERS THE GIFTS

In I Corinthians 12:1-3, Paul lets us know the purpose of the Holy Spirit. It's for us to have conscious control. Unlike the world, the Holy Spirit doesn't drive us into wild compulsive behavior!

Now we've established the gifts are a natural part of man – one's skills and abilities. The Holy Spirit is the gift Jesus promised that would transform and empower the body of Christ.

> *You shall receive power when the Holy Spirit has come upon you....* (Acts 1:8a)

> The Word clearly tells us that: *For we don't wrestle against flesh and blood, but against principalities, against powers, against the rulers of the darkness of this age, against spiritual hosts of wickedness in the heavenly places.* (Ephesians 6:12)

In essence, sometimes we're fighting against forces and powers we can't see.

There comes a point in every day life when we simply need a miracle. No matter how gifted we are we still need some extra help.

Miracle: Works of a supernatural origin and character such as couldn't be produced by natural agents and means. Miracles are also called signs or mighty works. A miracle is simply God superseding His own **laws**.

Law: A rule of conduct, recognized by custom or decreed by formal enactment, considered by a community, nation, or authoritatively-constituted group as binding upon its members; a system or body of such **rules**.

Rule: Controlling power, or its possession and exercise; government; dominion; authority.

Laws are given for the purpose of controlling people. The Old Testament law was given to man to restrain him from the evil tendencies natural to his fallen state. In other words, **the rules were given to keep us from hurting ourselves**. Whenever the government wants to control the population for whatever reason it comes up with new laws or amendments. Under the New Testament of Grace, we enjoy the benefits of the gift of the Holy Spirit.

> *The letter kills, but the Spirit gives life.*
> (II Corinthians 3:6b)

The law commands us to love or else. The gift of the Spirit transforms us to love because we want to. Love doesn't control and will not be controlled.

> *Now the Lord is the Spirit; and where the Spirit of the Lord is, there's liberty.*
> (II Corinthians 3:17)

No one wants to be controlled or forced to do something. Have you ever been in a relationship with someone who tried to force you into loving them or try to buy your love? **Love is a choice**. Jesus chose to love us and His desire is for us to choose Him. Jesus, like the Spirit, is a gentleman. He will not force Himself on you. Jesus said to the Samaritan woman that she didn't recognize the gift of God, but that the hour is coming when the true worshipers will worship in Spirit and in truth. (See John 4:10, 23)

The Spirit destroys the bondage of ignorance and enlightens us that we always have choices. The Word says the truth will make you free.

For example:

> Before I was Spirit-filled, I wasn't responsible for taking care of my son. I was threatened with child support and other negative pressures, but after being filled with the Holy Spirit, I wanted to do all I could for him.

As a musician deep into pursuit of my career, I stopped to take care of my son (and everyone was shocked). I was willing to do whatever it took. That wasn't me, but the Spirit dwelling within me.

> *A good tree can't bear bad fruit, nor can a bad tree bear good fruit. Therefore by their fruits you will know them.* (Matthew 7:18, 20)

The Holy Spirit literally empowers all the gifts. The Holy Spirit harmonizes the gifts and God's purpose for the person.

MULTIPLE GIFTS

> _Therefore I remind you to stir up the gift of God which is in you...._ (II Timothy 1:6a)

Notice that Paul is admonishing Timothy to stir up the gift, singular, not gifts. What he's speaking of is the Holy Spirit. Some of us have gifts of which we are unaware. The Bible speaks in terms that we can understand and relate to. The Scripture tells us in **I Corinthians 12:14** that the body has many members. Everyone is gifted and has access to all the members (gifts) by way of the Spirit.

For example:

> I'm a drummer and I use my hands a lot. People clearly see my hands working most of the time when I exercise this gift, but I have other body parts as well that I can still use. Just because I'm not utilizing them at that time doesn't mean I can't. When I was Spirit-filled on Sunday August 7, 1993, I found that I could do all kinds of things. I wasn't aware that I was an administrator, teacher and song writer. I don't mean hitting and missing. I mean with prevalence and power.

The Holy Spirit is a facilitator. He keeps us on the right track. By facilitator, I mean if I gave you a telephone or television set, but you had no means of power, what good are they? AT&T facilitates the telephone with lines. General Electric facilitates electrical appliances, but without power or access to power, the gift is null and of no effect.

Paul was telling Timothy to hook up to the power and utilize the provision that Christ died for. If we find that our gifts are dead, or we have no sense of direction or focus, we must stir up the Spirit (Power). God wants the saints to mature to the point that we pray and seek His face because we want to.

I remember going to the prayer room because of things I wanted, but after spending some time with the Lord and falling in love with Him, I couldn't stop praying. I can't imagine a day going by without talking to my friend, sharing my secrets and asking my Father for advice and counsel. I can't imagine what life would be like without Him in my heart.

I love giving Him all the glory and praise. I have discovered over and over again that in my flesh dwells no good thing. It's instinctive to thank Him over and over again for my gifts and opportunities and for His direction. I just can't stop praising His name. When I didn't believe in myself and felt I had to please everyone, He took me as I was. He still takes me as I am. Now I love Him because I want to. I need Him every hour, and when I can't speak or pray for myself, His Spirit speaks for and through me.

Your Gifts Are Not Your Purpose!

Chapter 3

YOUR GIFT CAN BUILD OR DESTROY YOU!

Your gift is personal. It's a tool that can build or destroy you!

Have you ever wondered why there's so much confusion centered around the entertainment and sports industries? Because people in this industry are either using their talents outside of God's intended purpose or they don't **understand** the purpose of the gifts in their lives. Not only will others exploit your talents when there's a lack of understanding or direction, but they will **pervert** you as well.

Perversion: to use outside of its intended purpose.

Our gifts are an asset, not a **curse**. When we use the gifts outside of their intended purpose, the outcome is **devastating**. One apparent outcome is **unhappiness** and unhappiness left untreated could lead to destruction.

I began playing drums at the age of eleven. At twenty-five, after a series of attempts to find my place in the entertainment industry, I decided to move to Los Angeles in June of 1987. It was, however, a bumpy and strange road that finally led me there.

37

My grand-aunt came to visit our family for the first time because of the death of her only sister, my grandmother. When I was about ten, my grand-aunt came to St. Louis where I was born. I was so happy to say that I had an aunt like all the other kids. All the neighbors knew me because I used to shovel their snow, cut their grass and run errands. I loved to **work** for some reason, but we will talk about this later. I believe because I was so kind to my aunt, she took an extra liking to me. When she left to go back to Omaha, I promised her I would write.

She asked me what I wanted for my birthday, which is December 19th, and I said a bicycle. She mailed me a ten-speed, which had just been introduced to the marketplace. It was like mailing a homeless child a house in Beverly Hills, even though I couldn't ride the bike because it was too large for me.

The following year she asked again, what did I want for my birthday or Christmas and I said, "a drum set." Again she bought the gift through her J.C. Penny's account. I didn't know how to set the drums up, but my brother Lamonte read the instructions and assembled them for me. I wasn't quite twelve years old when I took them to church and began playing **immediately**.

I will never forget my first night of rehearsal. As soon as I hit the drums, my mother ran out of the church. She was so nervous, because she knew I'd only had the drums for two weeks and never had a lesson.

As time went on, I started getting better. We attended a church called The Baptist Church of The Good Shepherd, were David Epley, a Caucasian man, was our pastor. David Epley was a well-known radio personality around the country. No matter where you traveled, if you turned on a religious station, you could find the radio personality of Pastor Epley!

Two things happened. One, I was exposed to a successful and well-known role model up close, something I never had. I was brought up in a family of nine boys and one girl. I was the sixth child and my mother raised the ten of us single-handedly. Second, David Epley became my idol. He sang, played guitar, preached, prophesied and prayed for the sick. He was also a cook and a great administrator. When I was almost thirteen years old, I noticed that Pastor Epley lost his drummer. Pastor Epley conducted revivals across the country and preached to very large audiences. Knowing he was to leave in a few days for New York, I asked if he needed a drummer and he said, "Yes." My first gig on the road was in Brooklyn, New York at the

Brooklyn Academy of Music, now known as B.A.M.

Time went on and I got better and better. Pastor Epley moved to Miami, Florida and built another church under the same name. I gained experience playing in local jazz and R&B (Rhythm and Blues) bands around town. I was always the youngest.

I went away to college at Doan College in Crete, Nebraska, where I was given a partial academic scholarship. After one semester, I returned to St. Louis and attended Webster College, (Webster University). They offered me a scholarship in music and I accepted.

Later, still searching for some stability, financially and emotionally, I joined the army. Two of my brothers had enlisted and it seemed to have a positive affect on their lives. I was also curious and willing to try anything once. I'm sure I was desperate and wanted to get out of the house. I needed consistent income, but I was also determined to accomplish my goals as a musician. The recruiting officer assured me that, after basic training, I would have a sure spot in the President's Band.

Well, of course that didn't work out and after basic training, I managed to get out of the army with an

Honorable Discharge. I was about twenty-one and I had lined up a lot of gigs for that winter. All was going well when one of the worst winters I had ever experienced hit St. Louis. It broke all kinds of records.

In January 1984, I decided I wouldn't spend another winter in St. Louis; all my gigs had been cancelled. After scouting around trying to decide where to live, I chose Atlanta. I went to scout out Atlanta and while there I called a friend who was the minister of music for David Epley in Miami. He asked me to come there.

In April or May of 1984, I moved to Miami, Florida. There I began playing for Pastor Epley's church in Miami. I asserted myself well and began playing music with bands for all the elite country clubs. Pastor Epley wasn't traveling as much, but after one year he went on television and wanted to contend in the Televangelism circuit. I began working in other capacities for his church organization called Good Shepherd Ministries. I learned how to book radio time, auditoriums, hotel arrangement, and much more. I moved very quickly in rank within his organization, but I found that I was unhappy. After becoming a successful businessman, I yearned for the struggle of a musician. Everytime I went out to eat or was around live entertainment, my heart gravitated toward my music peers. Yes, I had to admit to myself I was **unhappy**.

I felt as if I were **cheating**. I had to know if I could make it as a musician or not, I just had to know. So I left Miami after a little over three years and moved to Los Angeles in June 1987. For almost eleven months, I worked in every club, hotel, and church, anything I could get my hands on to try to get a shot at the big time. For the first time in my career, I felt I wasn't good enough. The answer I had to know, but feared the most, had come. I was extremely unhappy and lost what little self-esteem I had. I was planning to get married and when I lost the woman I really loved it was more than I could bear. I swallowed a bottle of sleeping pills and tried to take my life. I still remember it like it was yesterday.

I centered everything I had around my gift. I lived to play the drums when I should have allowed the drums to play through me. Music is a means of **expressing** what you are, but it's not who you are. Yes, your gifts can build you up or tear you down. I wanted success at all costs. I wanted success the way I wanted it.

> *This Book of the Law shall not depart from your mouth, but you shall meditate in it **day** and **night**, that you may observe to do according to all that is written in it. For then*

> *you will make your way prosperous, and then*
> *you will have **good success.*** (Joshua 1:8)

This well-known Scripture says it all. The law is God's righteousness or God's way. It says God's Word should not leave your mouth. We should apply the Word in every situation of our life. It says to meditate or continue to study, so you will know how, why and when to apply the Word.

Then you will have **success** you can enjoy. You will have **peace** of mind and you can enjoy the prosperity that the Lord has granted.

CHARACTER AND THE GIFT

Character:

No matter how successful you are, if you lack character it will amount to nothing. Poor character will tear down talent every time. Another reason we hear so many terrible things about the entertainment world is because performers are given so much at one time without being taught. As a result, relationships, money, clothes, people, and things have no value.

It was a blessing to have my aunt, but look at the story closely. I didn't have to do anything for the bike and when I received it I really didn't appreciate it. From there the process began. I became noted for my ability to play the drums and not for who I was as a person.

Success came too fast and I wasn't taught to be responsible for it. I should have been encouraged to make good grades and then given a bike. This builds good character.

For example, look at some of our role models:

> *Mike Tyson* in a heavyweight championship bout bites his opponent's, Evander Holyfield's ear on international television.

> *Dennis Rodman* of the Chicago Bulls spits on an official or kicks a camera man on national television. Rodman, one of the world's greatest rebounders for the prestigious Chicago Bulls, keeps his teammates and officials prisoners of fear by the outrageous behavior he may exhibit.

> In the same year The New York Knicks lost several players at a crucial point in the playoffs for **fighting**.

> *O.J. Simpson*, an American hero, was arrested on charges of killing his wife and Ron Goldman, exposing a long trail of domestic violence. What a tragedy!

The list of personalities given too much too fast is endless. Even Bill Clinton the President of the United States is haunted by character charges of outside marital affairs and ethical violations that mar his presidency. No matter how high you go, poor character will tear you down.

Jesus trained the disciples to continue His work. The root word for discipleship is discipline. A disciple is a follower and **learner** of Christ. It's not enough to go blindly after success, one must also be taught.

Tiger Woods at age twenty-one broke all kinds of records in golf. His father, a man with a military background, instilled strong character in Tiger. You don't see the wild and compulsive outbursts in Tiger Woods. His father, an ex-marine, taught him discipline. His father said, "After Tiger empties out his mind he can put his **pure** gift up to anyone."

Even basketball great Shaq, formerly of the Orlando Magic and the Los Angeles Lakers teams, attributes his success to his stepfather, whom he refers to as the General!

These men were taught good character and the results are evident. A person is not successful until he leaves **successors** behind. Jesus was the most successful man who ever lived. We are a product of His teaching.

DON'T CENTER YOUR LIFE AROUND YOUR GIFT

When we center our value or self-esteem around our gifts, our thinking becomes **distorted**. I don't have to elaborate on the arrogance of Hollywood or people with money and fame. But it's sad when that same spirit rests on preachers of the gospel.

It's amazing what money and fame will bring out in church people. Notice I said **bring out**, not what it does to them because they are already that way.

> *A good man out of the **good** treasure of his heart brings forth the good things, and an evil man out of the **evil** treasure brings forth evil things.* (Matthew 12:35)

I'm afraid many of our clergy are exploiting and manipulating the flock and it's not all the leader's fault. We follow others because of their talents, the way singing makes us feel, or to get a word from a particular man of God—as if God can only speak to him.

Our churches are running over not necessarily because we are being fed truth, but because of personalities promoted on television, crossover lyrics or the beat of the music. I've even witnessed preachers selling tickets to hear them preach the gospel. This is pure entertainment.

> *But go rather to the lost sheep of the house of Israel. Heal the sick, cleanse the lepers, raise the dead, cast out demons. Freely you have received, freely give.* (Matthew 10:6, 8)

The Scripture conveys that God gave Jesus to us for free and He taught us by example through His disciples. It cost Christ, not man!

We should not make celebrities out of servants. Everyone is gifted! You don't have to pay for oil, prayer cloths, prayer or anything else. The Bible says that Jesus paid it all, and we can come boldly to His throne. We must learn to apply **principles**, not **pay**!

Gifts are given for the edifying of the church, and when used outside of their intended purpose they promote something or someone else.

The Bible says a house divided against itself can't stand. No one should consider himself to be more worthy, more important, more deserving of salvation, or more essential than anyone else. Possession of different talents or gifts doesn't denote differences in worth, for all belong to one body, to one another, and all are interdependent. To think otherwise is to distort reality.

Everyone is talented! Everyone is special! Remember, we are made in God's image.

Image doesn't mean we look like God. It means we have the same characteristics as God. We have the ability to create, think, express and, most importantly, we have the power to choose. The power to choose sets us apart from God's other creations.

The sun can't decide to stop shining. The wind can't dictate when and where it will blow. The animals and every other entity of God don't have the free will of choice, but man has the power to choose. When you give that power away and seek after various preachers and teachers, healers and other forms of man, you throw that power away. Yes, they have their place in the process of our individual growth, but think about it. Would you want to be on insulin the rest of your life or a slave to the pharmacist or physician? The church is a spiritual hospital, but let's be well and live.

Jesus came that we may have life and that life more abundantly, not that we merely exist. When we choose to believe that God communicates in special ways, only with special people, this removes the responsibility for hearing God's message for ourselves. By listening to what others believe they've heard from God, you don't have to think for yourself. When you receive a message from God or His Word directly, then you're responsible for the interpretation.

> *Study to show **YOURSELF** approved, a worker who doesn't need to be ashamed, rightly dividing the word of truth.*
> (See II Timothy 2:15)

You are only a slave when you stop thinking, when you stop seeking God for **yourself**.

> *And don't be conformed to this **world**, but be transformed by the renewing of your mind, that you may prove what is that good and acceptable and perfect will of God.*
> (Romans 12:2)

This Scripture admonishes us to change our thinking. Once you change your thinking, you will prove what the will of God is for you.

Ephesians 6:12 tells us that we don't wrestle with the people we see, but the forces motivating them— principles of good versus evil—and these rulers will enslave us.

> *Let us therefore come boldly to the throne of grace, that we may obtain mercy and find grace to help in time of need.*
> (Hebrews 4:16)

You can come to God for yourself. Christ didn't die on the cross to leave you in the hands of just anyone. Christ certainly didn't give His life for the gifts, and neither should you. Don't center your life around your talents. Center your life around God, His love and His principles.

Love has to be free to love. Because if it's not free to love, its not true love.

Love is a *choice*. God loves you so much that He gives you a choice at the risk of you saying no to Him. Establish a relationship with the Lord for yourself. Jesus said, "If you love Me, learn of Me."

Christ is not coming back for religion. He's not coming back for the Baptist, Methodist or the Church Of God In Christ; although some in these denominations think they're the only ones going to heaven. I haven't discovered any scripture to support these claims. Christ is not looking for church folks! There are churches on every corner right next to 7-Elevens, liquor stores, motels and strip malls. Anyone can build and sit in a church. One of satan's favorite hang-out spots is the church.

51

Christ is looking for those individuals who want to build a relationship with Him.

YOU WERE NOT CREATED FOR THE GIFTS. THE GIFTS WERE CREATED FOR YOU!

Keep in mind that God has a desire to express Himself. I'm not saying God can't exist if this desire is not met, but God does have a desire to express His **glory.** (See Exodus 33:18-23)

The universe and this world which we live, express the glory of God. Even though God created the earth and man to express His greatness, God didn't create people for the earth. He created earth for people.

> *For thus says the Lord, Who created the heavens, Who is God, Who formed the earth and made it, Who has established it, Who didn't create it in vain, Who formed it to be inhabited: I'm the Lord, and there is no other.* (Isaiah 45:18)

God created Himself in order to enjoy, relate, and express Himself because He is the only of His kind. Remember, we are created in God's image, and the earth we inhabit.

> *And God said, "See, I have given you every herb that yields seed which is on the face of all the earth, and every tree whose fruit yields seed; to you it shall be for food. Also, to every beast of the earth, to every bird of the air and to everything that creeps on the earth, in which there's life. I have given every green herb for food." And it was so.*
> (Genesis 1:29, 30)

But God couldn't have a relationship with grass, trees, rain, birds, and such, because these natural elements don't have the choice to CREATE!

The nature of God is creativity! God's greatest expression of Himself throughout the universe, His greatest passion, is you!

> *What is man that You are mindful of him, or the son of man that You take care of him? You have made him a little lower than the angels; You have crowned him with glory and honor and set him over the works of Your hands.*
> (Hebrews 2:6, 7)

Like God, we have an instinctive desire to create. We also have a need for expression. God has provided the tools by which we can express ourselves. We are the managers of this planet. We can build, tear down and build again, but the greatest tool God gave us is to create with the gifts.

You were not created for the earth; you were not created for the gifts. Think about it. Gifts are designed for a lot of reasons, but I can't think of any gift I've purchased without having the person in mind. We are created to have dominion over the earth and to multiply. We are not created for things or privileges to have dominion over us.

Our gifts are a unique way in which we express ourselves. One reason so many people love the book of Psalms is because many of the Psalms were accompanied by music. Much can be expressed with the art of music; and, David, the well-known psalmist, used his gift of music to its fullest.

But, our existence testifies to the expression of God. Remember James 1:17 says, "**Every** good and perfect gift comes from above." I can't think of a gift more fascinating or perfect than the gift of life. Life is still our most puzzling expression of God. Whether you are a believer or not, your existence bears witness to God's glory.

Creativity is the free expression of every person. No matter who you are when you **express yourself,** you testify to the glory of God. Whether you acknowledge God or not, it will not change who God *is*.

My existence and ability to create bears witness of His glory, because I was created to express His glory, not mine. Whatever choices I make will not alter God's will for me.

> *The Lord has made all for Himself, Yes, even the wicked for the day of doom.*
> (Proverbs 16:4)

For example:

> *Now the whole earth has one language and one speech. And it came to pass, as they journeyed, from the east, that they found a plain in the land of Shinar, and they dwelt there. Then they said to one another, "Come let us make bricks and bake them thoroughly." They had brick for stone, and they had asphalt, for mortar. And they said, "Come, let us build ourselves a city, and a tower whose hope is in the heavens; let us make a **name for ourselves**, lest we be scattered abroad over the face of the whole earth." But the Lord said, "Indeed the people*

> *are one and they all have one language, and*
> *this is what they begin to do; now nothing*
> *that they propose to do will be withheld from*
> *them."* (Genesis 11:1-6)

This verse communicates that the people had one language and one speech. They were **focused** and once focused, they began to **create** to express **themselves**. This is natural because God created them to express His **glory**.

Second, God wanted to see their creation. Even though their purpose wasn't for Him, their **ability** bore witness of Him. Do you ever wonder why people who don't serve God or people who are not saved, tend to do better than those who are?

Sometimes it's simply a matter of principle. I just shared the story of the Tower of Babel to extract a principle. History teaches us principle, but God wants us to have an experience. I don't care what you've learned; it's just a principle on paper until the **Teacher** of all creation shows up in an **experience**.

God wants us to experience Him for ourselves. Even the principle of **faith** needs to be expressed. Everyone has faith, whether saved or secular.

God has dealt to each one a measure of faith....
(Romans 12:3b)

God placed every ingredient in man to ensure His invention of man. The manifestations of faith are **belief**, **hope**, and **trust**, but even this principle without experience is **useless**!

> *Faith without works is dead....* (James 2:26b)

Principles don't care who you are. One powerful principle is truth. Truth is so powerful, just a little of it will stand on its own.

For example:

> If I just pour a little water on someone it's going to have some effect. The person is going to get wet somewhere and water (truth) is going to find the lowest point (foundation).

Principles don't care about your religion, your background, sex, or ethnicity. If applied, you reap the benefit. For He makes His sun rise on the evil and on the good, and sends rain on the just and the unjust. Other people are successful simply because they apply the **principles** of God!

> *For whatever a man sows, that he will also reap....* (Galatians 6:7b)

57

When Ford created the automobile, it didn't matter what the consumer did after purchasing the care. Ford got the **glory** for the creation. The creation of human beings expresses the glory of who God is.

THE GIFTS AND BLESSING OF CHOICE

God gives us the ability to create and to express self. It's the express will of God that we choose Him. Yes, we are fashioned in the image of God, but it's only when we turn our gifts to Him that we give Him the glory He desires. The gifts are truly created to give Him glory.

King David was the greatest musician and song writer who ever lived, because he turned his heart and his gifts **wholly** to the Lord. We spoke of his son Solomon from Proverbs 16:4, however, Proverbs 16:3 says,

> **Commit** *your works (creativity) to the Lord, and your* **thoughts** *will be established.*

This says God will establish your very thoughts in **Him**. We spoke of the story of the Tower of Babel. However, because they were building a tower to themselves, God confused their tongue. God can't have a relationship with you if you choose only to have a relationship with yourself. Just imagine what would have happened if all those people at the time of the Tower of Babel were in one accord with God! God wants us to express ourselves in Him. We were created to worship Him and reflect His glory. In essence, God wants to look at you and see Himself as one looks into a mirror. We look in the mirror to see **ourselves**. Well, God wants to see **Himself** because we are made in His image.

If you don't think you enjoy looking at yourself, just count how many mirrors are in your house or surroundings. I mentioned earlier that the gifts bring either curse or blessing.

> *Oh, taste and see that the Lord is good;*
> *Blessed is the man who trusts in Him.*
> (Psalm 34:8)

Remember God has issued every man a portion of faith and the principles of faith are belief, hope and trust.

- *Faith* at its highest level is belief in Jesus Christ.

- *Hope* in all that has not happened and trust in His **promises**.

- *Trust in the Lord with all your heart, And lean not on your own understanding; In all*

59

> *your ways acknowledge Him and He shall direct your path.* (Proverbs 3:5, 6)

If you desire to maximize your gifts at their full potential, turn them back to their origin, it's natural to express something that was created for its purpose. Tell of His goodness and you will find that your soul will cry out **Hallelujah**. Yes, your soul is looking for an **experience** or an opportunity to express the glory of God.

God created those desires and you will not experience true fulfillment until you turn your **talents** to Him.

A large amount of this book was written while working in Europe. The more I traveled, the more I witnessed the glory of God's creation. I've discovered that, of all the monuments across the globe, the ones that stand out are those built to Him. Even men in their ignorance of God, when they thought they were building it to Him, put their souls into it. The blessing is when you choose to express Him through your gifts. I'm a living witness that when you stop serving the gifts and serve God, He will supply your every need.

On August 3, 1993, after losing the gig with George Benson and Bette Midler, I wondered what I was going to do. I had reached a career peak, and I had nothing to show for it. Everyone thought I was going to crack, but it was the Lord who directed me in what I thought was an unfortunate situation. I didn't know what to do. Somewhat in despair, I turned to Him again. This is so awesome because I couldn't understand why God would lead me to failure. It appeared as if I had it all. After auditioning and being chosen for an opportunity to perform with "The Divine Bette Milder" (as they call her), it was snatched away as quickly as it came.

> *Being **confident** of this very thing, that **He** who has begun a good **work** in you will complete it until the day of Jesus Christ.*
> (Philippians 1:6)

If I don't know anything else, I know I have a **relationship** with God and I communicate with Him daily, all day. And I certainly knew and know when He is speaking to me.

The Scripture says I'm to be confident it's not me doing the **work,** but God. So I went to a group at my church titled, Prayer and Bible Band. I was struggling with some habits and I wasn't Spirit-filled. I sought after the Holy Spirit, but for some reason, it never happened. A sister stood up during testimony service and spoke words that I really did not pay much attention to; but then she said,

"However, this kind doesn't go out except by prayer and fasting." She quoted Matthew 17:21.

This Scripture really caught my attention! I thought to myself, I have nothing to lose. It was Tuesday night, August 3rd and I decided to fast three days with just water.

This is how I addressed the Lord. I said, "God this is it, either You are going to fill me with the Spirit, deliver me from these **tormenting** habits or I'm going to stop believing in **You.**"

And, I heard the Lord say, "Okay, but you're going to have to do everything I tell you." I was suffering from insecurity, but I was a good actor. So often we try to control everything and everyone in pursuit of true identity. Even worse, we attempt to control God and dictate how He should direct our lives.

The Lord responded immediately to my plea. For the first time, I was completely honest with the Lord. I was angry with God, and I expressed those feelings to Him. And He began to show me that I didn't believe in Him as much as I thought I did.

Remember true faith is **trust.** So for the first time I was willing to surrender. I gave Him everything— every thought, my food, and my pleasures. I laid them all on the table and basically said, "Prove yourself Lord."

So I was led to give things away, stop seeing certain people, and approach strangers or people I knew would begin praying for me and affirm what God was about to do in my life. The second day of my fast I was in pain, angry, uncomfortable, and afraid, but I was determined. The Lord led me to share about fasting to my mechanic's wife. I was about to give up because the headaches were so painful. She pulled out a book entitled *Help, Lord the Devil Wants Me Fat*. She explained to me that after three days of fasting it becomes much easier. So, I was encouraged to go on.

Before I left the shop, the Lord said, "Go to her husband and allow him to pray for you." You see, I really felt I wasn't good enough for God. I had an overwhelming amount of shame regarding my past. Praying out loud or anything of the sort frightened me. I said, "No." The Lord said, "Well, if you let something this small stand between you and your request, so be it." I was caught in a catch-22. I didn't want God to have any excuses when this was over, so I yielded. These kinds of incidents (tests) went on all day. I was backed into a corner. It was Thursday night, and I testified earlier in noonday prayer what I wanted the Lord to do. You see, I decided to attend church every day at least twice a day. It was our regular Thursday night service. I could hardly stand on my feet.

A missionary/evangelist asked me if I would stay for an all night shut-in. It would begin that night until Saturday morning. I told her I couldn't stay up that long. She said just stay a few hours. I had always heard about the shut-ins, but never attended, so I felt I had nothing to lose.

I remained until about 1:00 a.m. and went home. It was Friday. I looked at my calendar (I still have it as a memorial) and I was so caught up in all the activity that I forgot I had a gig that night when I made a vow to the Lord.

I hadn't watched television or listened to any secular music. I didn't want God to have any excuses so I said, "Lord there's no way I can do this performance. I'm exhausted and I will have to play music." I decided to give up the whole thing. A friend of mine named Holli came over, and I shared with her all that had taken place. Holli wasn't a believer at the time, but the Lord used her to encourage me. She said, "It seems to me that if the Lord led you this far, then you should be able to finish it." I couldn't believe what she was saying, but it made sense. I was looking for an excuse to quit. I knew there would be temptation at this **event**.

When I arrived, the first thing I saw was loads of food. The band was scheduled to play there for three hours. This was true torture. After playing the first set, I talked to the bass player's wife. Only a few people knew I was fasting because I didn't want to boast about this consecration, but for some reason I shared it with his wife. She said that I wasn't supposed to tell people I was fasting. By now it was time to play just one more hour, and her husband commented that's why I played the drums so well, because of my spiritual nature. I guess his wife told him I was fasting.

After we finished performing, his wife said that everyone in the front of the stage was praying for me. I looked, and it was as if a circle of tables were around the stage. I shared with her that I was going to a shut-in at my church. I was so encouraged. It was about 1:30 a.m., and I was headed home. I thought finally this will be over, and I could eat, but more than that, I knew something was going to happen that night. I drove home slowly from Century City. It was the showdown I had long awaited.

About 2:00 a.m., while I was still heading home, the Lord was giving me instructions even down to the clothes I would wear that night—white shirt, a pair of blue jeans and sneakers. As if I was going to war, I knew something was going to happen. Driving home I thought about all that happened to me. It would take an entire book to express. I saw how it all made sense. The unloading, building of my faith in Him (hope), because I kept going and He kept sending people and situations. I knew that it was some kind of set-up. I was tired, but I was ready to face the music. On my way to the door, the Lord said, "Drink the water on the table." I looked and there was a half gallon of water. I was sick of water. If I drank one more glass of water I felt I would crack. I said, "No!" The Lord said, "You have come this far and now you want to risk it over a bottle of water?"

Angrily, I snatched the bottle of water and began drinking. It was horrible. As I walked to my car and I saw **Kevin**. Remember my friend, the only one who advised me not to take the Bette Midler gig. He asked, "Where are you going?" Still forcing water down my throat I said, "To a shut-in at my church," It was as if he appeared out of nowhere. He wished me well and I drove off. I got to church at 2:45 a.m. I drank the last of the water and went into church. It was time for the last corporate prayer. It was now 2:55 a.m., and I was on my knees at the altar and the Lord said to me, "Go tell the missionary to look at her watch **so you will know** when I deliver you." I said, "No! No! No!" I tried to pray and I couldn't. All I kept thinking about was, "Suppose this hinders

God from answering my prayer." So I went to the missionary and told her.

I got back on my knees and lifted my hands to heaven and yelled "Hallelujah" until I couldn't say it anymore. I felt as if a lightning bolt went straight through my body and knocked me to the floor. This is the miracle everyone witnessed. The Lord answered my prayer.

That following Sunday, August 7th, Bishop Blake preached and asked whoever wanted to be filled with the Holy Ghost to come down to the altar. Before I could get to the altar, I was filled. It was an **experience** I will never forget. The Lord created a circumstance so that I may have an experience to believe, trust, and hope in Him for myself.

The Lord said that I would never have to audition for anything again. Several years have passed, and I have played for some of the greatest artists in the world. Remember Kevin? As days went on, he kept saying there was something different about me. Others witnessed this remarkable transition as well. Kevin went on to record two CD's. He asked me to play on both of them. He received a Grammy for the second CD.

Let me share with you how God works. It was Kevin Moore **(Keb-Mo')**, that afforded me the tranquility and travel in Europe to write this book.

God used every person I had come in contact with during the Bette Milder situation. God allowed me to **live** *Your Gifts Are Not Your Purpose*. It's when I lived for Him that He allowed everything I wanted to come, when it didn't matter anymore.

We give power to the enemy when we place value on the gifts. When I decided I didn't have to play, then playing the drums presented itself to me.

Don't live for your talents. Allow your talents to live through you.

My pastor always says, "If I never had a problem, I never would have known God could solve them."

Thank you, Lord, for Bette Midler.

Your Gifts Are Not Your Purpose!

Ch4pter

YOUR GIFT IS A VEHICLE TO YOUR PURPOSE

A man's gift makes room for him, and brings him before great men. (Proverbs 18:16)

This is one of the most liberating Scriptures in the bible. Much principle and direction can be extracted from it. The author of this passage King Solomon was the wisest man who ever lived. God says in I Kings 3:13, there hadn't been anyone like him before nor should any arise after. I Kings 4:31 states King Solomon was wiser than all men.

Proverbs was probably written when King Solomon was mature and at the height of his power. Solomon shares how to prioritize one's **values**, values which lead to good character, character that leads to wholeness, and wholeness that provides satisfaction. Solomon, like his father King David, was extremely gifted. It was Solomon, not David, whom God allowed to build His **Temple**. This honor and awesome responsibility was granted to Solomon. So Solomon relays this timeless treasure: **your gift** (singular) **makes room for you**. Solomon, like many of us, had several gifts, but I believe he was speaking of one's primary or natural gift, the gift that brings you popularity, fame and divine favor.

71

Solomon was an administrator, king, and poet to name a few of his gifts, but he is best known for his gift of **wisdom**. People traveled from all around the world to witness his wisdom.

For example:

> *[1]Now when the queen of Sheba heard of the fame of Solomon concerning the named of the Lord, she came to test him with hard questions. [3]So Solomon answered all her questions; there was nothing so difficult for the king that he couldn't explain it to her. [6]Then she said to the king: it was a true report which I heard in my own land about your words and your wisdom. [7]However I didn't believe the words until I came and saw with my own eyes; and indeed the half wasn't told me. Your wisdom and prosperity exceed the fame of which I heard.*
> (I Kings 10:1, 3, 6, 7)

Kings, rulers and many other people went to witness King Solomon's primary gift of wisdom. Everyone is blessed with a primary gift, but many people confuse their natural gift with their purpose. Solomon's primary gift attracted much attention, wealth, and power.

For example:

> You see a black Mercedes. You are aware of its performance (fame), its value or prestige (wealth), and now you want to test the car for yourself. During the test drive you become impressed with its capabilities. It has a state-of-the-art sound system, rides smoothly at super high speeds, comfortable seating, driving flexibility, a sun roof, high profile rims and tires, and much more (talent). Even with all the luxury and refinement of a Mercedes, its primary purpose is to get you from point A to point B (drive). The average person goes to test drive a new car without inquiring if the car runs or not, because we assume the purpose of a car is to be driven.

We love talent! Your talent is simply a means (vehicle) to your purpose. You know that it was God's grace and the gifts that brought us out of many horrible living circumstances.

As I mentioned before, I grew up with nine brothers and one sister, all of whom my mother raised alone. We lived in a housing project and attended public schools. During my eighth year in public school, I clearly remember learning nothing, because the teacher spent so much time disciplining the other students. Most of my peers experienced the same

73

living conditions as I did, or worse. Our futures appeared grim, and our circumstances measured us to fit right in with negative statistics. Against those odds, I started playing the drums and I found myself in favored positions. The better drummer I became, the more exposure I attained. I'm sure you know of other success stories like this.

The scripture says your gift will make room for you. That means literally your gift will move any obstacle. All you have to do is work on your craft (gift). Your gift was given to you by the Lord and that's why it's called a gift. God is perfect and so is your gift's ability to move any obstacle.

> *For exaltation comes neither from the east nor from the west nor from the south. But God is the Judge: He puts down one, and exalts another.* (Psalm 75:6, 7)

Listen, you don't have to prove anything to anyone. Stop trying to promote yourself and allow God to do it. God has already made provisions for you through your gift. Remember I shared with you that the Lord told me I would never have to audition again. God will secure you; you don't have to fear anyone. That's why church politics are so horrible. Politics mean that you have to please people in order to get a position. Politics promote feelings of instability or fear of what others may think, never being able to stand for one's true beliefs.

I'm not encouraging you to smother your gifts. I'm saying allow God to promote you in His time. God's not looking for ability, but availability. Let people know you're available and allow God do the rest.

If God was looking for ability when he delivered the children of Israel out of Egypt, He would have chosen Aaron. Aaron was a good speaker even according to God, but God chose Moses because of his humility. There are some who are gifted in humility.

Don't allow fear to sponsor your motives. Allow love to sponsor your heart. The Scripture says your gift will make room for you. It goes on to say, and brings you before great men. Let's look at the second half of the Scripture. It says, "and brings him before great men." Wherever you need to go, don't worry about it. Your gift will literally pick you up and take you there.

As a musician, I've had the opportunity of traveling all over the globe, while being compensated for the experience. God, our greatest teacher, will provide for every necessary **experience**. After receiving the Holy Spirit, I wanted to quit because I stumbled so many times, but I couldn't get over the experience I had that night during the church's monthly shut-in when the Lord touched me! The Lord touched me in an incomparable way. That experience keeps me holding on to His promises. Going before greatness brings about exposure.

The Prophet Samuel anointed David to be king when David was around seventeen years old. David didn't become king until age thirty-three, but the Lord used his spiritual gift (musician) to place him before King Saul, whom David would replace. David's gift made room for him.

Joseph was sold by his own brothers to merchants on their way to Egypt. Joseph found himself in prison and it seemed everyone had forgotten about him, but the Pharaoh had a dream that no one could interpret and the cook remembered Joseph and told Pharaoh. Joseph interpreted the dream and became what is equivalent to Vice President of Egypt. Joseph's gift (interpreting dreams) made room for him.

Your gift can move any obstacle. Your gift can and will also pick you up and transport you wherever you need to go and to whomever you need to go before. Your gift is on assignment and can't fail.

> *Therefore I remind you to stir up the gift of God which is in you....* (II Timothy 1:60)

Paul is exhorting Timothy, who is a little timid, because he is young and inexperienced, and appeared not up for the fight. Because of his soft nature, having been raised by two women (II Timothy 1:5), Timothy needed to stir up the gift. Paul is telling him to stir up the Spirit, and the Spirit will give him direction and guide his spiritual gift. You don't have to be afraid of anything, for:

> *God has not given us a spirit of fear; but of power and of love and of a sound mind.*
> (II Timothy 1:7)

Don't allow people or anxiety to run you crazy or cause you lose your focus. Relax in God. The pressure is not on you, it's on Him. You didn't ask for the gift He invested in you. So just be thankful for what God is doing through you.

When Adam and Eve sinned, it wasn't hard, to see; they were afraid, and hid from God. Fear gave them away! God never gave them or exposed them to the spirit of fear. A perfect God didn't instill you with gifts to frighten you. He designed those gifts to bless you.

Does it grieve you when you invest in your children's education only for them to drop out of school? When you instill values in your daughter, but she winds up pregnant? When you prepare your children for a career, but they end up quitting? I wonder how God feels about his investment in you.

God will see to our every need. He has assigned your gift to facilitate your mission.

YOUR GIFT FACILITATES YOUR PURPOSE

Let us not confuse our natural gift with our spiritual gifts in the Body of Christ. What I mean is that your primary gift works for you. It has been assigned to you, for you. It facilitates your needs. Your gift is your life-long tool. I'm a writer, so I will need writing utensils—pencil, paper, typewriter, computer—to facilitate my writing. I will always need some kind of tool to facilitate this talent.

I'm a drummer and, I need drums and sticks. The tools don't change the gift, its ability or potential. However, these tools are necessary to play my instrument.

The more familiar I become with the tools (sticks, drums, pencil, paper, and computer) the better I can express and communicate what I want to say. The more understanding I have of these instruments, the more effective I will be.

In all your getting, get understanding....
(Proverbs 4; 7b)

The Scripture admonishes us to get an understanding. It says in all your getting, meaning whatever you're trying to achieve, allow understanding to be your primary pursuit. So many errors and calamities center around the gifts for lack of understanding. Ignorance is the enemy's tool in many areas of our lives. The Lord says, "My people are destroyed for lack of knowledge." (Hosea 4:6) Imagine serving the God of the universe! He is the God who owns it all, and you're called not just a servant, but His child. When we lack knowledge, we operate in confusion which affirms procrastination.

> *In all labor there's profit, but idle chatter leads only to poverty.* (Proverbs 14:23)

There's no reason for a child of the King to be in poverty. How is it that people sold out for God, seeking Him with their whole hearts suffer in so many other areas? Sometimes it's simply a lack of knowledge.

> *A scoffer seeks wisdom and doesn't find it, but knowledge is easy to him who understands.* (Proverbs 14:6)

Abuse is inevitable when one lacks understanding. We must utilize the one tool God gave us all, **our minds**!

WORKING THE GIFTS

Whether rich or poor, old or young, black or white, saved or bound, no matter how much understanding you have nothing happens without work. More times than not, many suffer from poor work ethic. It's unnatural not to work. The proper universal word for work or the divine usage of this institutional principle is creativity. As I mentioned earlier, our souls crave an experience, but the tool which facilitates this natural desire is work or creativity. The two words are interchangeable.

Work at its full potential, I believe, is creativity. Creativity involves working. If God has anointed me to share anything else, this is certainly it. If you grasp this concept, you are on your way to freedom in every area of your life.

Now, everything about God encompasses work. The very nature of God is to work, which can be summed up in one word, creation or created.

- **Created**: To form or fashion, to produce, to create.

- **Creating**: By bringing into existence and by fashioning existing matter into something new.

God in His totality went to work to bring forth the world in which we live. We find God at work in Genesis 1:1. In the beginning God created the heavens and the earth. And the Holy Sprit was at work in Genesis 1:2. The earth was without form, and void; and darkness was on the face of the deep. And the Spirit of God was hovering over the face of the waters. And we find Jesus at work in John 1:1-3. In the beginning was the Word, and the Word was with God and the Word was God. He was in the beginning with God. All things were made through Him, and without Him nothing was made that was made.

Every dimension of God went to work to create vegetation, animal life, and people. Not only did God work, but He worked hard. He worked six days before He stopped creating. Keep in mind these are six working days in heaven.

And on the seventh day God ended His work which He had done, and He rested on the

> _seventh day from all His work which He had_
> _done._ (Genesis 2:2)

When God said, "Let Us make man in Our image, according to Our likeness" (Genesis 1:26), He imparted in you the same nature to create. If the God of all creation worked, what makes you think you don't have to work? Working is synonymous with living. There's a blessing in working. Working is a universal principle.

> _Then God blessed the seventh day and_
> _sanctified it, because in it He rested from all_
> _His work which God had created and made._
> (Genesis 2:3)

God was pleased with His work so He blessed Himself and sanctified the seventh day. It was as if God had a party with Himself. The Scripture says He was pleased with Himself. **Sanctified** means to set aside. So in essence, God ordained (appointed) the seventh day to observe and celebrate His creation, whether you believe in the Sabbath or not. Whether it's Sunday or Saturday on your calendar, God has set aside a day to celebrate His creations and, if you attend the party, you will partake in the eternal blessing.

Sometimes God will bless you in your going, and He most certainly blesses the obedient. Let me put it in traditional terms so as not to offend anyone. God ordained the Sabbath day, and those who observe it share and enjoy the divine blessing of God. Our gifts make room for us. The gift facilitates our purpose and working activates our gift.

Yes, our gifts work on our behalf. Our gifts are certainly assigned to us; for nothing we do can change the nature of the gift. We may change, but the gift remains on schedule. The gift will take us before great men (facilitate) if we will believe and let talent do its part, but we must exercise the gifts. Working is man's personal instrument.

God worked six days supplying tools for man to work with, and for everything around him. When something is not working, it's considered of no use or of little value. When the body begins to decay or stops functioning, the process of death is in effect.

> *Now in the morning, as He returned to the city, He was hungry. And seeing a fig tree by the road, He came to it and found nothing on it but leaves, and said to it: Let no fruit grow on you ever again. And immediately the fig tree withered away.* (Matthew 21:18, 19)

Working brings forth productivity. What good was the fig tree if it yielded no fruit? What good is a car if you can't drive it? What good is your gift if you don't use it?

> *Do not neglect the gift that is in you....*
> (I Timothy 4:14a)

What a tragedy if God who imparts so much in you and me, found us producing nothing? I don't want to be found in that predicament, and sentenced to destruction.

> *Jesus said, "I must work the works of Him who sent Me while it's day; the night is coming when no one can work."* (John 9:4)

Jesus said **He must work**. He only has so much time. He must utilize His time and gifts wisely. I believe Jesus knew how much time He had, but you and I don't. So the need for diligence is all the more crucial.

You know the story of Samson and Delilah. An angel of the Lord revealed to Samson's father Manoah that he would have a son. Manoah asked the angel what would be the boy's rule of life, and his work (see Judges 13:12). Samson's father wanted to know his son's purpose and his.

Yes, child of God we suffer, from lack of work ethic. You will find the principle of work in more Scriptures than you realize.

It's when you study that you present yourself approved to God, according to II Timothy 2:15. By study, He means work. Creativity entails working. Work brings glory to God and God blesses you His ultimate creation.

Only after God finished creating was He ready to share the most intimate part of Himself. That moment occurred when the Creator breathed into man's nostrils the breath of life. God enjoyed man most after He finished creating. Not only does God celebrate creation, but you will find Him most intimate when you are working for Him. This creative side of man is called worship. Worship involves work because our flesh doesn't want to work.

> *For I know that in me (that is in my flesh) nothing good dwells; for to will is present with me, but how to perform what is good I don't find.* (Romans 7:18)

Paul is saying that it's a struggle to serve God. Paul the Christian, one of the leaders of the church, says he's struggling. Paul says there's something else pulling him (will). Paul is saying to serve and truly worship the Lord takes effort.

The great worshiper of all time, King David, said *"I will bless the Lord at all times; His praise shall continually be in my mouth."* (Psalm 34:1)

David is saying no matter how I feel, no matter where my flesh wants to take me, I will bless the Lord. I will work through every situation no matter the circumstances.

So, as you can see, it takes a made-up mind and a working spirit, soul and body to serve the Lord. I will discuss this further in my next book.

Life and work are synonymous. Everyone, everything, all the universe, sun, moon, and stars are working to show forth God's glory and majesty. Our gifts were created for praise and worship, not only for man's glory, but for God's.

> *Laziness casts one into a deep sleep, and an idle person will suffer hunger.*
> (Proverbs 19:15)

The Scripture tells us that laziness promotes complacency. A lazy person will become conditioned to an idle lifestyle. This person will probably suffer. When we choose not to exercise

our creativity in whatever areas in our lives, we suffer. If you don't work to stop cigarette smoking, you suffer. If you're a poor steward of finances, you will surely suffer these days. If you chose not to exercise your craft, it will probably lose its effectiveness. The Bible says, *Work out your own salvation with fear and trembling....*
(Philippians 2:12b)

Don't complain if you are not willing to work. God won't do anything for you that you can do for yourself. When Peter was thrown in jail, the Angel of the Lord put the guards in a deep sleep. The Angel unlocked the bars, but the Angel told Peter to stand up. Peter stood up and the chains fell off him. Then the Angel told Peter to put his shoes on his feet. The miracle was the chains falling off and the opening of the prison doors. The blessing was when Peter was obedient and exercised what he could perform.

Obedience requires work on our part. I've already discussed that faith without works is dead. God, often times, will not perform a miracle without your participation.

If anyone will not work, neither shall he eat.
(II Thessalonians 3:10b)

The scripture speaks for itself. I don't understand how people feel they should be served all their lives. Worse are Christians who feel God should serve them for nothing. Everything costs someone something. Nothing is free from sacrifice, but let us take this principle scripture further.

If one just has to experience hunger, hunger and thirst for righteousness! Laziness takes on the mindset that people owe you something! The mindset of the homeless is universal. I was standing in line to experience the Eiffel Tower in Paris, France, and a homeless woman put her hand out for money. I gave her some change and she asked for more. When I didn't give her more money, she left angry with a horrible attitude. Sometimes we damage people when we encourage them to beg. We are sending mixed signals that it's alright to beg, but begging or hustling takes work. That energy can be channeled into positive self-productivity. It's a blessing to work. We bless the Lord when we create.

JESUS THE ENTREPRENEUR

We must not confuse working with having a job! I can't find the word "job" anywhere in the scriptures. I found the character Job, but not the word "job." Job is a system that man created to keep people impoverished. A job is not necessarily creative.

Think about it. How many people get up everyday to work for someone else? Look at all the large corporate takeovers and acquisitions. Various corporate institutions want to corner the work market. You would think they would encourage the Mom and Pop store. Now that would liberate people to control their financial destiny. Look at history. The principle of slavery centers around free labor. Free labor or forced labors' objective is to produce wealth for someone else.

It takes no creativity because you do what people tell you or command you to do. Slavery in its truest sense is to smother the power of choice or thinking, thus stifling creativity.

Nothing has changed. For example, Latinos are pouring over the Texas and California border to flee impoverished conditions. Corporations as well as others exploit the desire of Latinos to have a better way of life. Most of these people are underpaid, doing meaningless jobs, but it's alright because Americans want free or cheap labor. Now several of our borders are overwhelmed with more people than we can handle.

Think about it. How many of YOU go to work everyday dreading every moment of it?

When you are employed, you work toward the dreams and ambitions of others. You count their money, cars, boats, homes, vacations, and so on. I want you to think about how you feel after spending time doing the same thing over and over again.

Punching a computer for someone else has to get boring. Chauffeuring someone else around in their car when you don't have one after a while has to become frustrating.

You will find more and more there are fewer incentives for starting your own business.

I went to MacDonald's in Switzerland, and I noticed cashiers don't have to count change anymore. They have buttons for hamburgers; buttons for french fries, soda, and a button that determines how much change to give the customer. Corporations are making it easier to get cheap labor. Cheap labor means you don't have to think.

That is why slave owners didn't want African Americans to read because once you read you begin to think. If you ask questions, it ignites your imagination, you begin to create.

There's no reason that every child of God shouldn't have their own business. Whether large or small, this is God's will for you.

It's alright to have a job to gain experience, but you don't have to die in the same place. Today, that's hard to do. If you don't assemble some skills in the twenty-first century, you will find yourself a slave to the system. Systems are designed to keep control over people. America is a great country for this reason. People migrate from all over the world for the same reason. The Constitution was created on this principle. It's still the most attractive aspect of this country. **It's freedom of expression and freedom of speech**. Show me a place where people are free to express themselves and I will show you massive creativity and diversity! Often, what we call a job is just another name for slavery. A job will showcase your ability, yes, and creativity, but it will be for the enjoyment of the slave master.

Jesus is the best entrepreneur who ever lived.

> *Don't labor, for the food which perishes, for the food which endures to everlasting life, which the Son of man will give you, because God the Father has set His seal on Him. Then they said to Him, What shall we do, that we may work the works of God?*
> (John 6:27, 28)

We should ask ourselves how we can follow the entrepreneurial work plan of Jesus Christ.

91

> *Jesus answered and said to them, "This is the work of God, that you believe in Him whom He sent." (John 6:29)*

To simply believe in Christ Jesus and to live and follow His teachings, enrolls you into business school for self.

> *And Jesus said to them, "I'm the Bread of Life. He who comes to Me shall never hunger; and He who believes in Me shall never thirst." (John 6:35)*

Jesus has the best contract for success that time can buy. The fine print says you'll never go hungry, and never thirst. Jesus is success; Jesus is not the right thing to do, but He is the only way to do it. I'm speaking from experience. I didn't have consistent male role models in my life and as I grew older I really got into the teachings of Christ.

Don't be intimidated by the tricks and deceitful systems of this world. Jesus has all the answers in every area of your life, especially business. I have never failed when applying His principles. Man will give you insurance, but Jesus gives you assurance!

The Samaritan woman at the well was looking for love in all the wrong faces. She was trying to work out her unhappiness on her own terms. Jesus said to her he would give her water that she would never thirst again.

Jesus is not only the best example of an entrepreneur, but He has a training program as well.

Before Jesus performed any miracles during His mission, He assembled a staff and trained them. Jesus called His staff "**Disciples.**"

For example:

> *And Jesus, walking by the Sea of Galilee, saw two brothers, Simon called Peter and Andrew his brother; casting a net into the sea; for they were fishermen. Then He said to them, Follow Me, and I will make you become fishers of men.* (Matthew 4:18, 19)

Jesus recruits His first staff members, but He calls them to leave their occupations. In order to follow Him continuously, they will form a new society, be formally appointed and sent out on a mission.

It's difficult to follow the teachings of Christ and remain an employee. Jesus wants you to deploy yourself. Jesus in essence shared with His disciples how to be self-sufficient. God wants you to mature in Him that He may use you to the fullest. This principle applies to every area of your life.

It's funny when you share with others your desire to work for yourself, they will attempt to talk you out of it. Amazing, isn't it? What's more amazing is resistance that comes from family or friends.

> *And He said to them, "Why did you seek Me? Did you not know that I must be about My Father's business?"* (Luke 2:49)

Some will not understand your drive or passion to express yourself for yourself. Don't waste a lot of time trying to convince people of your desires, hopes and dreams. Once you try to win the approval of others, compromise is inevitable.

Destiny was driving Jesus at age eleven or twelve, and His mother and father didn't understand Him. You don't have to live out the dreams of your parents or anyone else. God has gifted you with your own unique destiny!

Jesus will also instruct you on how to conduct yourself in the workplace. When you start your own business, you will receive a lot of rejection at times. Don't allow it to discourage you and don't take it personally.

Don't start doubting yourself. Stand on God's Word!

> *And whoever will not receive you nor hear you, when you depart from there, shake off the dust under your feet as a testimony against them....* (Mark 6:11a)

You have nothing to prove. Your gift will make room for you. Stand on the promise. When you stand on God's Word, you bring glory to Him. Christ came that we may have life more abundantly. Christ didn't lay His life down for you to be an impoverished saint. This will not bring glory to God. This doesn't reflect His promises. It certainly doesn't bring Him pleasure. Would you enjoy seeing your children that way?

> *Beloved, I pray that you may prosper in all things and be in health, just as your soul prospers.* (III John 1:2)

Talent will literally take care of you financially; especially if you turn your gifts to Christ. There's no reason that every child of the King should not have his or her own business. This is God's perfect will. It reflects the true nature of God.

> *I have glorified You on earth. I have finished the work which You have given Me to do.* (John 17:4)

God gave you the gift you have. Utilize it to the fullest and I guarantee that your primary gift will bless you and activate all the other gifts to the fullest. Then you will truly reflect the creative God of the universe.

Begin—**NOW!** I admonish you. Don't allow fear to sponsor your procrastination. Surround yourself with successful people, those who will encourage you. Surround yourself with people who are active in the things you would like to do.

You are not too old and you are certainly not too young. Your gift is on assignment!

Chapter 5

SO WHAT IS PURPOSE?

So, with all the examples of Scriptures and my own personal experiences, whether spiritual or practical, with so much emphasis placed on one's primary gifts, YOUR GIFTS ARE NOT YOUR PURPOSE!

Though my talent afforded me many experiences, without purpose or destiny, experience is just a roller coaster of continual trial and error.

In Jeremiah we read:

> *Then the word of the Lord came to me, saying; Before I formed you in the womb I knew you; Before you were born I sanctified you; I ordained you a prophet to the nations....* (Versus 4, 5)

The Scripture tells us that before our parents ever thought of us, God knew us. Remember, no matter what choices we make, every person's origin is God. The Scripture goes on to say that God sanctified him. Sanctified meaning set apart. God created you and me, then He set us apart for something. That something is called **purpose**. God didn't create us just for the fun of it.

A father certainly wouldn't have a child just because he has nothing to do. Even with unplanned pregnancies, before the child is born, plans have to be made for its welfare. Certainly, God wouldn't create you and allow you to go through all your pains and trials for nothing.

The Scripture goes on to say He ordained Jeremiah a prophet to the nations. To ordain is to appoint one to a position in life.

All the problems, ups and downs, good and bad experiences—all lead to Jeremiah's purpose: to equip him for the position as God's prophet.

God has set you aside because He appointed you long before you were born. Purpose, very simply, is the reason God created you. I don't mean me, but you. It's an individual thing. You must discover God's purpose for yourself. If you want to discover the true reason for living, you must consult the Creator, the original source of your existence.

You are not an accident. Don't buy into the lie that you are an accident or a mistake. Your parents may not have planned for you and they may not have wanted you when you arrived. They could have changed their minds once you were born. Even if they hoped for a boy and got a girl, prayed for a girl with all their heart and you're a boy, that's who you are supposed to be!

When a man and woman apply for a life (sexual intimacy), it's either granted or denied. Yes, we do choose whether or not to have children, but God, the source of all creation has the final say no matter what the circumstances.

For example:

> I read where Minister Louis Farrakhan's mother tried several times to abort him. No matter what your feelings are about him and his beliefs, God granted his life.

Many people desire children and would probably make great parents, but for some reason God denies their request. Others are truly considered unfit parents and yet children are placed in horrible circumstances. Only God knows the reason. It doesn't change who God is. His ways are past finding out.

So don't listen to anyone telling you that you are a mistake. Don't buy into that negativity. It's an old trick of the enemy. Exercise your gift and you will walk into your purpose. Purpose is something we feel we can't do. I'm sure like me, you thought at some point in your life: **Why doesn't God just reveal things at the onset?** Well, if you look back, you'll realize that when God asks us to do some of the simple things, we say "no!" We feel it's too hard or we're not good enough.

Often we fear what others will think. We are afraid to fail in the presence of others or want the approval of others.

If we look further in Jeremiah 1:6, Jeremiah says this to the Lord! *"Ah, Lord God! Behold, I can't speak, for I'm a youth."*

Jeremiah, like most of us, felt he was unqualified for the position. If God had revealed His purpose to Jeremiah sooner, he would probably have messed things up.

But the Lord replies to him (verses 7 and 8):

"Don't say, I'm a youth, for you shall go to all to whom I send you and whatever I command you, you shall speak. Don't be afraid of their faces, for I'm with you to deliver you, says the Lord."

Notice God says; don't be afraid of their faces. Don't worry about what others think. God has set Jeremiah apart and appointed him. God has set your life apart and has a work for you. We've established when God created you; He placed in you the ability to fulfill your purpose. You have to realize, your purpose is His purpose working through you, and those tools or vehicles are the gifts.

When I began speaking, I felt no one would listen to me. I was terrified of reading a Bible verse. But my true fear was being rejected by others. My reputation was horrible. I was embarrassed about my past. I was my worst enemy, but God is saying to us as He said to Jeremiah in verse 8: *For I'm with you to* **deliver you.**

God is aware of your past guilt and shame. Remember, He knew you before you were born. He knew all the wrong choices you would make to get you in all the right places.

God began the process of delivering me from myself, so He could use me to deliver others. It didn't matter what I thought. Most people are not sure what they are supposed to do anyway, and become uneasy when left to face misery alone. Even if it means afflicting a husband, wife or family member, misery loves company.

So often we listen to others before listening to God. Much error would be avoided if we would simply obey Him.

> *Has the Lord as great delight in burnt*
> *offerings and sacrifices, As in obeying the*
> *voice of the Lord? Behold, to obey is better*
> *than sacrifice.* (I Samuel 15:22)

It doesn't matter where you are morally, God is speaking to you. Whether by His Word, dream, song, circumstances, conscience or simple instinct, God is speaking to you. Will you heed? Now, if you really want to be honest, sometimes purpose is something you don't want to do (God's will).

For some sin is pleasurable. If they listen to anything God says, the first thing they have to do is stop. Before you can listen, you have to stop long enough to hear God; and, for many, to stop is to stop sinning.

To do God's will, whatever it is, will entail being responsible and, as we said before, irresponsibility is slavery.

The worst kind of slave, however, is a slave conscious of sin. It's one thing not to know, but quite different when you know that sin is killing you and you are unwilling to stop.

For many people it's easier to enjoy the ups and downs and pains and bruises of sin. So they function in blatant denial! Some simply don't want to change.

An abnormal life has become comfortably normal. Temptations will always be there, but the power of choice is ours as well.

For example:

> When the time came close for Jesus to be offered up on the cross, just for one moment He started to change His mind. The disciples (friends) had fallen asleep on Him when He needed them the most.

> *Saying, "Father, if it is Your will, take this cup away from Me; nevertheless, not My will but Yours, be done.* (Luke 22:42)

Jesus knew it wasn't God's will for the cup to pass. That would abort His purpose. Jesus, unlike most of us, was aware of His purpose early in life. He was influenced by the pain of His friends' lack of support.

But when God calls you to teach, exhort, preach, pray, dance, heal, sing, serve, and so on, not only will He give you the ability, He also will provide the place and people to minister to.

105

I will never forget in 1994 our church conducted a symposium, and I was asked a couple of weeks prior the event to teach a class. I was scheduled to teach a class already with another musician, but I believe a space opened up and our Executive Minister of Music said the Lord wanted me to instruct another session.

Of course I said "no." She was insistent, so I went to the Lord and asked should I instruct the class, I heard nothing from the Lord. Time was running out, and Sister Judy was still pushing. The next day I went to 6 a.m. prayer and it came to me that I promised the Lord I would do whatever He wanted me to do. There was no need to pray about whether to instruct the class or not, because I had already promised to do His will. I was looking for an excuse; so I went to her and said "yes."

Then she wanted my outline. I thought, **"What will I teach?"** The other class was already outlined for me.

I thought about a sermon I'd preached once, but it wasn't in lesson form. So I patterned my outline after some of the others from the year before.

The day finally came for me to instruct the class. It was a Saturday afternoon. I felt no one would attend. Most people didn't know who I was, and the ones who did saw me only as a drummer.

On my way to the class I saw all these people heading in the same direction. I asked the guard where all these people were going. He said, "To your class." He said, "The title sounds interesting and, I would like to see your notes."

I walked in the door and the class was full. I couldn't believe it. Oh, yes the title was *"Your Gifts Are Not Your Purpose!"* My intentions were never to speak or teach any class, but as I thought back I could recall standing in front of the mirror preaching with a broom. I used to walk down the street and pretend I was on my way to a big auditorium to speak. I was only kidding around and imitating others I saw. Little did I know that God had planted something there.

NOTHING CAN HINDER GOD'S PURPOSE

God's purpose is not hindered by our past. He used Moses who was a murderer. He used a prostitute named Rahab to assist the Children of Israel to possess the Promised Land. This harlot later married an Israelite and found herself in the lineage of Jesus Christ (Matthew 1:5).

God used the apostle Paul who tortured and took part in killing God's people. Paul helped establish the Christian church and dominates the New Testament.

Nothing you've done can cancel your purpose. Purpose will usually benefit the lives of others. Purpose gives you confidence. There's no greater feeling than knowing that you're doing the will of God. Purpose preserves you until it's accomplished.

> *I know that You can do everything, And that no purpose of Yours can be withheld from You.* (Job 42:2)

I remember an earthquake we had in California. I wasn't afraid; I actually said to myself, "I can't die, I haven't preached yet." Even in denial I knew sooner or later I would preach. I never thought it would turn out like this. What an interesting journey.

I never dreamed of writing a book. I didn't enjoy writing or studying. I remember completing my homework assignments early so I wouldn't have to take them home with me. But here I am, praising God and loving it. I thank God for all my experiences.

I try to relax and take my time in all my decisions because provisions have already been made for me.

> *Be anxious for nothing, but in everything by prayer and supplication, with thanksgiving, let your requests be made known to God.* (Philippians 4:6)

Another earth-shaking Scripture! Be anxious for nothing, not for success, failure, marriage or career. **God says nothing** and we certainly can't rush God.

The Philippians passage continues:

> *And the peace of God, which surpasses all understanding, will guard your hearts and minds through Christ Jesus.* (Verse 7)

God's peace which you can't fathom will guard you in all the provisions God has provided on your behalf.

If you relax in His purpose, you will experience His never-ending peace. No one including you will understand how you've made it, but God.

Chapter 6

GOD'S MULTIPLE PURPOSE

God has a multiple purpose for everyone. I call them the 3CP's: *Created* **Purpose,** *Commissioned* **Purpose and** *Corporate* **Purpose.**

We've discussed a little what creative or individual purpose is and we'll get back to this later.

Individual purpose is the reason God made you.

What is **Commissioned** Purpose? In Mark 16:15, Jesus said, "Go into all the world and preach the gospel to every creature." This Scripture is called the Great Commission, because the work is great and it's expected of everyone. It's God's intention that no one be lost.

In its authentic origin (man's pre-fallen state) God intended this principle to be the rule for mankind.

A few years ago, I started a business entitled Caution Music Agency. We booked talent for venues all across the country. As our business grew rapidly, I had to acquire additional help. As an incentive I shared fifty percent of the profits with each booking agent. In other words, the agents were working on commission.

111

Jesus the entrepreneur said, go out and recruit clients for the Kingdom. Christ is in the business of saving souls.

> *Then He said to His disciples, "The harvest truly is plentiful, but the laborers are few. Therefore pray the Lord of the harvest to send out laborers into His harvest."*
> (Matthew 9:37, 38)

A recruiting agent in the Kingdom is called a Disciple. The Great Commission involves discipleship.

The greatest work one will ever do is to win someone to Christ. By this I mean to introduce others to Christ and His teaching. The Disciple's commission is love, joy, peace and eternal life with Jesus.

What is Corporate Purpose? Corporate Purpose: Psalm 69:34, *"Let heaven and earth praise Him, the seas and everything that moves in them."* The earth and all its dwelling were created to praise and worship God.

The universe and its vastness work in concert to express the glory of the Lord.

The awesome process of redemption (to bring man back to God) works toward the master plan of God's totality.

When I see a house, I know there are windows, doors, rooms, and appliances, but all I see is a house!

What's fascinating about a choir is though many choir members sing, dance, direct, and play instruments, when in their assigned place they all function as one. We call this harmony.

Humanity and all the elements that surround us, visible or invisible are part of God's eternal symphony.

How often do you hear people speak of individuals as special or unique and you feel left out? Even with all the talents you obviously possess, you still feel left out.

Or you may be someone who feels you have no skills at all. The little things you do are often overlooked or seem insignificant to you. Let me say again that all God's creations are special and unique.

Think about it. How can the God of perfection create anything other than that? Anything out of heaven is brilliant, even satan. God utilizes satan to bring glory to Himself. God uses the negative so we will appreciate the positive. One must put the things of life in perspective.

I'd like to illustrate how everyone including you, the ordained reader, is very special.

In order for me to prove why you're special, I will need to show you how you continue to overlook your own uniqueness.

You abort or smother your uniqueness when you stop being **yourself**. It's really that simple. The moment you stop following the footsteps of others and follow the footsteps of Christ, your uniqueness will jump out at you. Even if you don't follow Christ at first, your personality and character will come forth.

I'm not saying you'll be comfortable with who you are at first, but it will come forth and you'll find that it was there all the time.

Second, stop listening to others and listen to yourself. To thine own self be true. You're probably saying, "I can't listen to myself because I will continue to mess things up."

How do you think others discover themselves? They experience their own trials and errors. Even as an advocate for Christ you have to experience something in order to effectively witness to others.

When you truly get tired of pretending and being all the people you see, then go ahead and be yourself because—your true self is waiting to be expressed!

Your inner man knows you are a fake and your inner man is tired of being lied to.

> *He is a double-minded man, unstable in all his ways.* (James 1:8)

James communicates when you can't make up your mind about who you want to be, then you are unstable in not some things, but in everything you do.

When you choose to live your life in the shoes of others, you will question everything about yourself. What torture and mass confusion.

Listen, you can't help how you were created, the color of your hair, eyes, skin, your size, family, or where you were born. But if you go ahead and be yourself, I promise you that everything will be alright. How can I make that promise?

Because a perfect God created you for a perfect reason in this perfect time of your life.

> *For we are His workmanship, created in Christ Jesus for good works, which God prepared beforehand that we should walk in them.* (Ephesians 2:10)

The only reason that one wouldn't function as oneself, is selfishness. To be exactly as you want, how, when and where you want to be would make you God! There would be no reason for His purpose for you and His desire to be met through you!

> For He says to Moses, *"I will have mercy on whomever I will have mercy, and I will have compassion on whomever I will have compassion. So then it's not of him who wills, nor of him who runs, but of God who shows mercy. For the Scripture says to the Pharaoh, For this very purpose I have raised you up, that I may show My power in you, and that My name may be declared in all the earth. Therefore He has mercy on whom He wills, and whom he wills He hardens. You will say to me then, "Why does He still find fault? For who has resisted His will?" But indeed, O man, who are you to reply against God? Will the thing formed say to Him who formed it, "Why have you made me like this"? Doesn't*

> *the potter have power over the clay, from the same lump to make one vessel for honor and another for dishonor?"* (Romans 9:15-21)

The Scripture says it all. Yes, God gives us choices, but our choices will not replace or undermine God's authority. For example, how many times have you heard the old saying over and over by parents, "I brought you in this world and I will take you out!"

Does it bother you when you pay rent and someone tries to tell you what to do in your home? Imagine everything you have worked for or created and someone tries to dictate what you're supposed to do with it. God's will is perfect in your life. No matter what mistakes you've made, He will get the glory one way or another. He is God!

You are at your best when you are yourself.

> *Because you are lukewarm, and neither cold nor hot, I will vomit you out of My mouth.* (Revelation 3:16)

Jesus admonishes us to be honest with ourselves; be either hot or cold.

You see when you are cold or when you go ahead and drink, smoke, and function in immorality, you are a perfect vessel which God can use. Jesus can clean you up or fix whatever the problem is. In all reality, it's not a problem, just an opportunity for God.

It would be better to just go on and sin until you get tired, and make up your mind who you want to live for. God is not interested in lukewarm people. The Scripture conveys God will vomit you out of His mouth or His very presence.

I believe that when one continues to pray inconsistent prayers, God is not listening. It's when you say, "Here I am, Lord", that He will take you just like you are.

Even in rehabilitation, the first requirement is to admit what you are. Rehabilitation can't begin until one admits he or she is an alcoholic, or whatever the habit is. So if you're a bus driver, trash man, usher, cook, liar, cheat, swindler—whatever the case may be, you're still special.

God hates sin but loves the sinner. God doesn't always like what you do, but He sure loves you.

Being special simply means to just be yourself, because yourself is who God created, no matter what you are or what anyone else thinks. Life gets easier for you, for your sanity. Peace and focus line up when you decide to be yourself!

SEPARATING GIFTS FROM PURPOSE

The gifts themselves are sometimes confusing. It's easy to see how one could settle on the gifts and place all their eggs in one basket. The gifts are a great indicator of purpose, but *your gifts truly are not your purpose.*

Your individual purpose is the single reason God created you. It's the one thing that holds your entire life together.

For example:

> Nelson Mandela is a lawyer and a fighter, but being a lawyer wasn't the reason he was created. His skills as a lawyer clearly facilitated his purpose. He was jailed for his rebellion against the apartheid system in South Africa. He continued school and kept the movement alive even while in prison. You see, they can put you in jail or prison, but they can't lock up your soul and spirit. As long as you have faith, hope and trust you are alive.
>
> Mandela was jailed for twenty-seven years, but like so many other great men, he did more in prison than most of us free would ever do in a lifetime. Yes, Mandela was destined for

prison. Part of his purpose was prison. He couldn't fulfill his purpose free. His imprisonment focused global attention on the unfair practices of South Africa. Mandela couldn't fulfill his destiny without uncomfortable circumstances, but Mandela walked out of prison a free man. He went in to prison as a political prisoner and came out president of South Africa.

His very name Nelson, was given to him on his first day of school. Mandela was seven years old when he received his English name (Christian). The very people who oppressed him and his people are now under his authority and national jurisdiction.

David was a warrior, musician, song writer, poet, prophet, and father. David's spiritual gift was music. It was this talent that afforded him the opportunity to play before King Saul. David found favor with Saul after playing for him and driving out evil spirits that possessed the King.

> *So David came to Saul and stood before him. David loved him greatly, and he became his armor-bearer. Then Saul sent to Jesse, saying, "Please let David stand before me, for he has found favor in my sight." And so it was, whenever the spirit from God was upon Saul, that David would take a harp and play*

> *it with his hand. Then Saul would become*
> *refreshed and well, and the distressing spirit*
> *would depart from him.* (I Samuel 16:21-23)

But even with the anointing to play the harp that would drive evil spirits away, David's spiritual gift wasn't his purpose. David was chosen by God to be King of Israel. David's individual or created purpose was King of Israel.

Well, if you're still not convinced, how about Jesus? Jesus was the best human example while wrapped in flesh the world will ever know. If you want a perfect role model, example, rehearsal, or type, Jesus is it.

Jesus possessed all the gifts. He was a teacher, carpenter, healer, preacher, prophet, administrator, but even with all the gifts Jesus possessed, and all the power He had access to, even the Lord Jesus Christ's gifts, were not His purpose.

Jesus created, commissioned and corporate purpose were all wrapped into one. Jesus' purpose was to die on the cross for the sins of the world. He died that we may have life more abundantly.

Imagine your sole purpose is to die. Your only reason for entering into this life is to die for all mankind's mistakes. Jesus' gifts were not his purpose either and if Jesus' gifts were not his purpose, neither are yours. Like Jesus, you will have to die, but not for the sins of the world.

> _And we know that all things work together for good to those who love God, to those who are called according to His purpose._
> (Romans 8:28)

HOW TO DISCOVER PURPOSE

You might be saying to yourself, "What is my purpose?" So many wander through life asking themselves that same question! Some of you have sat in church, Spirit-filled, working in ministries and auxiliaries in so many capacities. You still don't know your individual purpose, or you think you know but you're not sure.

I would like to give you three clues that I'm sure will help point you in the right direction. The clues are **serving, need** and **love**.

I've spent the earlier part of the book explaining the gift and its purpose and how one must work the gift. We've established that one's primary gift works for self. We've established that one's primary gift (natural gift) is personal and a facilitator of one's needs in life.

The gifts are resources placed in the church to be utilized at the point of need for ministry. But what about the people who are gifted and don't attend church? Let's face it. Some are never going to church, and many of our brilliant minds are not going to the traditional church, but the operative word here is **need**.

> *And my God shall supply all your need according to His riches in glory by Christ Jesus.* (Philippians 4:9)

We must remember that God is the God of **all** creation.

> *The earth is the Lord's, and all its fullness, the world and those who dwell therein.* (Psalm 24:1)

God is the God of good and bad, right and unrighteousness, and God will see to the needs of His investment. God has supplied the doctors, lawyers, government, scientists, archeologists, teachers, philosophers, and builders. Whether they give Him the credit (glory) or not He has allowed the know-how and technology to go forth to secure His creation.

But let's get back to one of our operative words, ***work***.

Most people don't enjoy working because most people have a **job** that's unfulfilling. I would like to point out the most fulfilling work of all mankind—volunteering.

Volunteer: One who enters into any **service**, especially military service or a hazardous undertaking, of his own free **will**.

Volunteer: Springing up naturally or spontaneously, as from fallen or self-sown seed: To offer, to give, or do.

Yes, purpose centers itself around **need**. Purpose is to volunteer one's **service** without getting paid.

Service: To work for, especially as a servant. To be of service to; wait on, to promote the interest of; aid, help to obey and give homage to: to serve God. To be suitable or useable, as for a purpose!

A person is truly great when a person facilitates the perpetuation of humanity.

> *Yet it shall not be so among you; but whoever desires to become great among you, let him be your servant. And whoever desires to be first among you, let him be your slave – just as the Son of Man didn't come to be served,*

> *but to serve, and to give His life a ransom for*
> *many.* (Matthew 20:26-28)

Our greatest example, the perfect teacher, Jesus Christ came to serve mankind.

The church at times, functions in error. The bishops, clergy or whatever titles man has created should be seen serving, not being served.

One of America's most charismatic presidents, John F. Kennedy said, "Ask not what your country can do for you, but what you can do for your country."

When one enlists as a servant, one takes on the title **Minister**.

Minister: One who is authorized to administer the sacraments, preach, **conduct** services of worship.

One appointed to head an executive or administrative department of a government.

You don't have to have a title on the church roll in order to become a minister in the institution of service. One also doesn't have to be licensed. Just serve your brother and sister everyday and you are on your way.

Ministry: the profession, duties, length of service; the duties or function of a minister or body of ministers.

Life is a ministry in itself. It's a matter of choice in regards to whom or where you are going to serve.

Truly service is the ultimate ministry and should be the goal of all persons. You don't need a church to serve God, or to establish your ministry (service).

Before the Children of Israel had a temple, they worshipped God with the temple they were created with.

> _Or do you not know that your body is the temple of the Holy Spirit who is in you, whom you have from God, and you are not your own?_ (I Corinthians 6:19)

I'm not trying to speak badly about the traditional church and its leaders, but I would like to shed some light on the confusion. How can someone call himself a missionary without a mission? How can the church feed the hungry if we only feed at the church facility? Most of our Christian walk takes place outside of the church facility.

Ministry causes people to smile, laugh, love, pray, have hope, care, find understanding, spend time with the Lord and others, mother, baby-sit, work in shelters, give medical care, counsel, and much more.

This is the ministry Jesus is speaking of. Most of His ministry was in the streets with the common folk. Love is **servant**-inspired.

> *For you, brethren, have been called to liberty; only don't use liberty as an opportunity for the flesh, but through love serve one another.* (Galatians 5:13)

Love is servant-inspired. The selfish will never understand or accept this call. A servant is one who accepts and acknowledges a place beneath those who he serves, one willing to forsake the systems of social status on our human scale of values.

Servers are viewed as performing the unworthy tasks considered beneath those who they serve. Jesus says that those who function as His servants, will be honored by the Heavenly Father.

True servants will ultimately be honored by the one whom they serve and who has promised them honor for that service.

There's very little about society and our world that promotes serving today. Love is the motivator of true service. One can be gifted with a multitude of talents, but without love it amounts to nothing. It's just loud drama.

The greatest service is to serve God and His people. I'm not saying that one should not get paid or there's something wrong with becoming wealthy.

This is one of the reasons it takes many so long to discover purpose. Our primary gifts are personal and they serve our needs. But after you've made it and become successful, you will find that true fulfillment is to give back. It takes most a lifetime, but it doesn't have to take a lifetime to share with and serve others.

Purpose is centered on *serving* a *need* in *love*! Because when one truly matures and hungers for righteousness, **love will serve his need**.

> *Blessed are those who hunger and thirst, for righteousness, for they shall be **filled**.*
> (Matthew 5:6)

Fulfillment is the result of doing the will of God! Purpose is God!

Your Gifts Are Not Your Purpose!

Chapter 7

TIME

It's impossible to grasp purpose without gaining a proper understanding of time.

Time is purpose!

So what is time and how does it relate to purpose? Time in its truest sense is endless. Man in his purest sense (spiritual) is endless as well.

> *He has made everything beautiful in its time. Also He has put **eternity** in their hearts, except that no one can find out the work that God does from beginning to end.*
> (Ecclesiastes 3:12)

How does this relate to purpose? Well, purpose is like reading a novel and jumping to the end or peeping as many of us do when we read, but after peeping or scanning through the pages, you can't grasp the story until reading the entire novel.

Think of it as a producer at home working on a movie and the producer has determined who's going to play what part (chosen). These chosen characters are given a **script** once they **agree** to play the **roles**.

Remember the root word of Scripture is **script**. A lot of us just haven't taken time to converse with the author and finisher of our faith!

> *The end of a thing is better than its beginning; the patient in Spirit is better than the proud in Spirit.* (Ecclesiastes 7:8)

The operative word here is ***thing***. Thing can be translated event, season, time, space, but it's not the end of all. By all I mean the part of you that's endless.

> *To everything there's a season, A time for every purpose under heaven: A time to be born, A time to die; A time to plant, And a time to pluck what is planted; A time to kill, And a time to heal; A time to break down, And a time to build up; A time to weep, And a time to laugh; A time to mourn, And a time to dance; A time to cast away stones, And a time to gather stones; A time to embrace, And a time to refrain from embracing; A time to gain, And a time to lose; A time to keep, And a time to throw away; A time to tear, And a time to sew; A time to keep silence; And a time to speak; A time to love, And a time to hate; A time of War, And a time of peace.* (Ecclesiastes 3:1-8)

Time is broken down into three categories: eternity, time and seasons. Eternity is the part of time in which we originate. It's the endless aspect of time. Eternity is God because it's the consumption or sum total of all existence.

Time is simply—*Time as We Know It*, meaning it's the space in eternity that an earthly person functions.

Season is time divided into parts for a particular reason. Season is an **appointed** time called summer, winter, spring, and fall.

Season is the part of time that is directly related to purpose. People confuse seasons or purpose because they don't look like we expect them to.

For example:

> Just because the appointed season, winter, has come doesn't mean it has to be cold. It can be hot. Spring may not always bear rain for May flowers, but it is spring just the same. Whether you like it or not, whether it looks like it or not, spring is coming and there's nothing anyone can do about it.

So time is simply **space** carved out of eternity for man's **existence**. Seasons are broken into four parts called for an appointed time.

There's no such thing as running out of time. Time as we know it is running out of us.

IT'S NEVER TOO LATE!

It's **never** too late for you, I mean **never**. You are not too old to fulfill your purpose, and you are certainly not too young.

Abraham was seventy-five years old when he discovered, or God revealed, his purpose. Jesus was twelve years old when he began walking in His destiny. Now is your time!

Purpose truly comes down to one **source**, the Creator of all, **God**!

In order to reap and understand the full effect of your individual purpose, you must consider the source seriously. I don't know your background, but the Lord has appointed this season for you to read this message.

I encourage you to try Jesus. If you haven't, what do you have to lose? I promise you – nothing.

Whatever your hang-ups are about Him or whatever you have heard, try Him for yourself.

This is your time to fulfill your call. You have nothing to fear but fear it self. Love stands waiting with open arms.

God loves you far more than you can ever imagine. Who do you think gave you all those dreams, desires and ambitions? That's right, God did.

You just have to give Him a chance to give you some direction; that's all. It's nothing hard. No magic, no jumping over a broom or standing in some special line in church. Just get some counsel from the Producer so you can understand your script in life.

> *Looking unto Jesus, the author and finisher of our faith....* (Hebrews 12:2a)

And if you do know Christ Jesus, but have lost your way or thinking about giving up all together, now is your time to truly live. The Lord still loves you no matter what you've done. The Lord, like a concerned parent, just wants to hear from you.

He wants to tell you He loves you Himself in His own way. Your relationship that you've built or are going to build is so unique.

I would like for you to take this time and stop right where you are and speak to the One who loves you more than you'll ever know.

I'm not going to orchestrate your words for you. I'm not going to lead you in a sinner's prayer. No one knows your situation, your dilemma like you. You're the best person for this moment.

If you are angry, share that with God. If you're confused, don't talk to God like He is somewhere in outer space. You are made in His image; you are a part of Him. Go ahead, I'll wait.

Express yourself to Him. I only ask one thing of you. Put away all your differences and if you have never addressed Jesus, address Him now.

Focus your prayers on Jesus and conclude them in the name of Jesus. *Go on, we can stop here*. I know from this point on, your life will never be the same. I'm not saying something to you because I heard it. As you've read, I speak from experience.

I don't have to know your name or face to say to you that I will pray for you and your renewed or new relationship with Jesus, the rest of our lives.
May God grant you all the desires of your heart, for His desires are yours.

To schedule Minster Belle for speaking engagements or seminars, contact:

CARING MINISTRIES
5850 W. 3RD STREET, SUITE 353
LOS ANGELES, CA 90036
www.caringministries.com
(323) 957-4820

Or e-mail: lwbelle@hotmail.com

I would love to hear your questions or comments.

REMEMBER, WALK IN YOUR PURPOSE!

Printed in the United States
58582LVS00002B/22-51